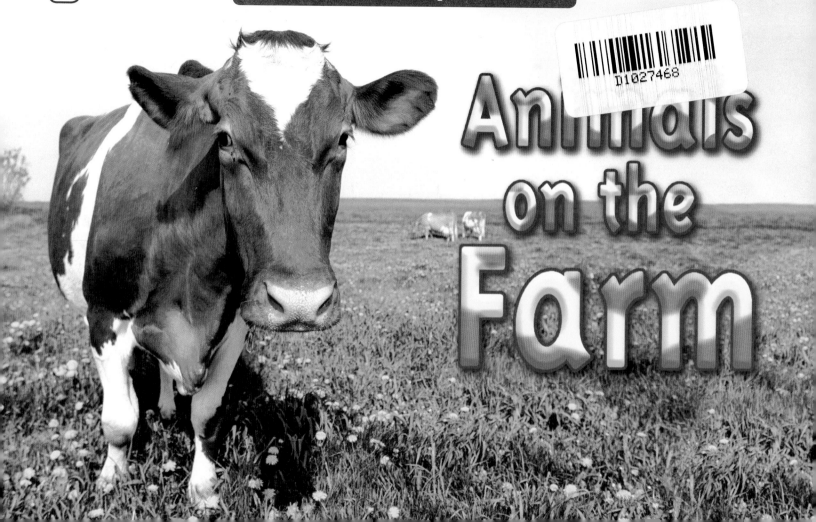

Animals on the Farm

Count the sheep.

How many sheep are there **in all**?

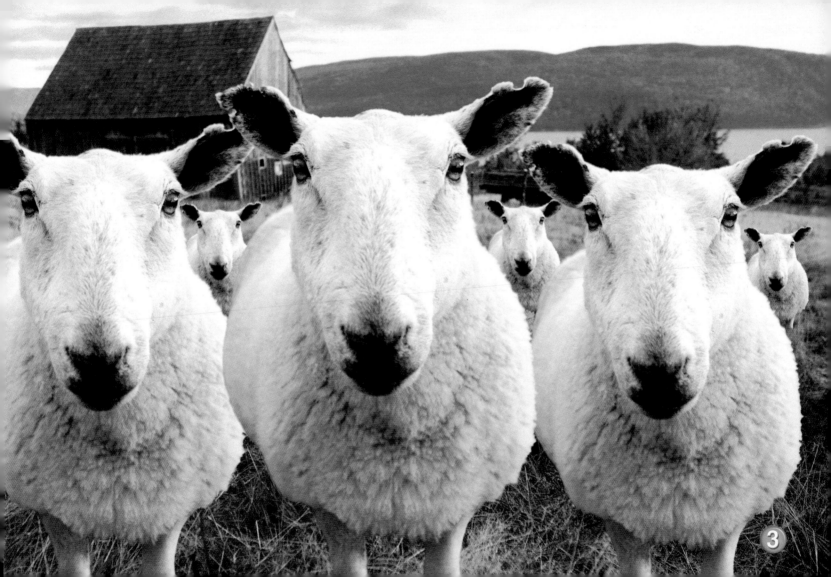

Count the horses.

How many horses are there **in all**?

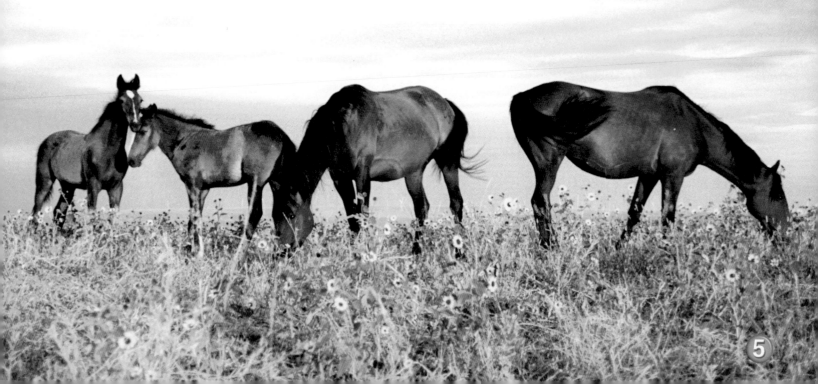

Count the chicks.

How many chicks are there **in all**?

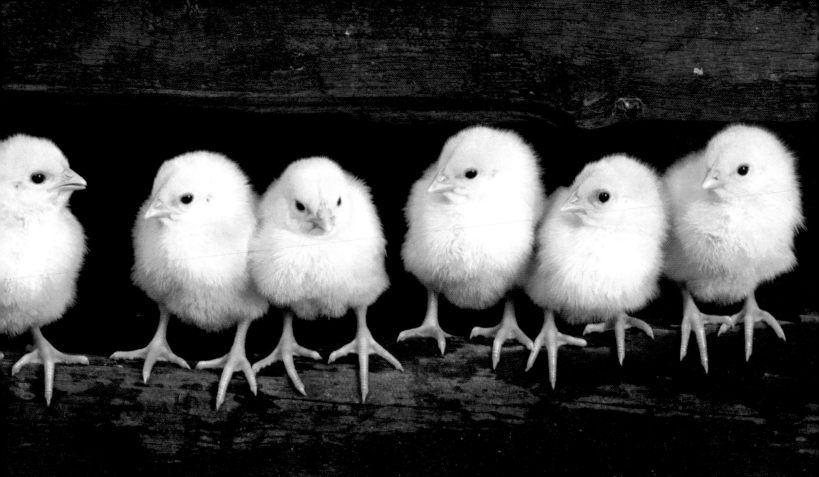

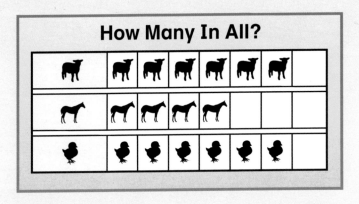

How many animals are there **in all**?